TRAIN
ACTIVATE
UNLEASH

THE PROPHETIC
Volume I

Dorothy Hisatake

TAU: Train.Activate.Unleash – The Prophetic Volume 1

Copyright © 2019 Dorothy Hisatake

Scripture quotations, unless otherwise indicated, are taken from the Holy Bible, King James Version.

Cover design:

1122 Teofilo Productions

(415) 948-1333

TABLE OF CONTENTS

Acknowledgements

I would like to acknowledge my Apostle and husband Eighi Jr. Hisatake for his love and guidance. Thank you for covering and guiding us as we fearlessly stepped into the unknown. No words can describe how much you helped me grow in the prophetic realm. Thank you for establishing the prophetic culture in No Limits Worship Center and in our everyday lives. Thank you for believing in me when I didn't believe in myself. I love you forever!

To the 5-Fold Ministry Gifts of No Limits Worship Center: Prophetess Regina and Pastor Legalo Haro, Pastor Penani and First Lady Lili Poloai, Evangelist Dora Uiagalelei, Minister Carol Neemia, Minister Steve Winn and the prophetic teams that are rising up for such a time as this. Your faith is out of this world, I have been so blessed by your anointed preaching, words, visions, dreams and revelations. You helped me search the deeper things of God and expand our gifts as we built upon the rock of revelation bringing everything together to build God's Kingdom. Words cannot express how much each of you has blessed my life. You all are truly unstoppable!

To the Prophetic Minstrels: Steven Finau, Malaki Hisatake, Zechariah Haro, LJ Scanlan, Mike Scanlan, Elijah Hisatake, Jr. Tolo, Rueben & Julie Igafo, Jaireh Leapaga, Mana Letele-Fiso, Ruta Letele Taliaoa, Lomiga Fualau & Pook; You minstrels clear the path for the prophetic atmosphere to be released. Your sound is pure and powerful. We couldn't release anything in the atmosphere without you. Thanks for going ahead and tearing down every wall! You are mighty warriors for Jesus.

To the Prophetic Worshippers at No Limits San Francisco (SF), No Limits Sacramento (SAC) and No Limits Revival: You all have a unique sound and style! Thank you for going with the flow and singing the word of the Lord with us without any practice; your faith blows my mind! Worship Leaders; Steven, Psalmists Miracle, Faith, Flora, Subrina, Mana, Ruta, Destinee, Allison and Vanna! God is moving! All I can say is ACCELERATION! Thank you for taking us higher in worship!

To the Prophetic Intercessors: My Mama Leano Vaovasa, Mama Aunoa, Mama Niu, Mama Tupu, Prophetess Regina, Sisters Carol, Daffy, Melissa, Lakisha, Porsche, my son Michael and daughter Mana. Thank you for sacrificing your time to pray and intercede for the people of God. Your hours of praying, travailing and standing in the gap is bringing in the harvest! My beloved mother Fa'aete'ete Tupolo, although you are not here your prayers are forever over us!

The Prophetic Armies of Lord: The youth and young adults at No Limits Worship Centers. It is such a blessing to see you step out and sing, dance, prophesy and share your visions and dreams! You have been called and chosen. You are destined for greatness! I'm excited for you and godly proud of you all.

To My Prophetic Company: My sons Eighi III, Elijah, Joshua, Malaki, Judah, Jabez and daughters Rain, Princess, Jazztina, Moetoto and Victoria; thank you for your love, insight, strength and courage. My granddaughters Pualani & Melony: you were chosen from the belly to praise, preach and prophesy! Love and appreciate all you do for our family!

PRAYER

Father God, I pray that this book will help to stir up every gift that may lay dormant in your people. I pray for knowledge, wisdom and understanding to what you have in store for those reading. May the prophetic winds blow through each page, may the window be opened to the prophetic dimension that every reader will see past the glass and touch and feel your fresh winds blowing upon them. I bring into remembrance past prophecies, dreams and visions. I unlock what's been hidden behind every door and loose the authority to access and walk through what's been closed. Lord I pray that the strategies in this book may be helpful and resourceful to your Kingdom in whatever area they are building. I pray that you give revelation and confirmation to every word spoken directly to them. I pray an increase of hunger and fire would burn in every soul. Hide me and let them see and feel you through these pages. Bind up doubt, confusion and fear and loose boldness, power, love and joy in the Holy Ghost. Let us walk and step out and build, edify and encourage the saints by the prophetic gift in us. I seal every page with the blood of Jesus, In Jesus Name Amen.

To Jesus my master and King, I love you! Thank you for saving me and choosing me; you found me when I wasn't looking for you. Since my encounter with your light in 1997 you still light up my world. My life belongs to you. Speak Lord; your servant is listening!

DEDICATION

I dedicate this book to my Polynesian brothers and sisters; I write from my heart that this book will stir up the gifts that may lay dormant with you. Our culture is one of servant hood, commitment, humility, love, respect and honor. A people where our ancestors put God first and he is our foundation. Prayer and worship is our lifestyle and the Man of God is held at the highest place of honor because he is the servant of God to the people. I honor you and I know God has so much in store for you. It's your time the people of the ocean!

Isaiah 41:1 KJV Keep silence before me, O islands; and

Let the people renew their strength: let them come near;

then

let them speak: let us come near together to judgment.

Acts 2:18 NLT In those days I will pour out my Spirit even

on

my servants men and women alike and they will prophesy.

INTRODUCTION

Proverbs 25:2 KJV It is the glory of God to conceal a thing: but the honour of kings is to search out a matter.

Daniel 1:17 KJV As for these four children, God gave them knowledge and skill in all learning and wisdom: and Daniel had understanding in all visions and dreams.

Isaiah 48:6 NLT You have heard my predictions and seen them fulfilled, but you refuse to admit it. Now I will tell you new things, secrets you have not yet heard.

Job33:15 AMP "In a dream, a vision of the night (one may hear God's voice), When deep sleep falls on men while slumbering upon the bed.

Deuteronomy 29:29 KJV The secret things belong unto the Lord our God; but those things which are revealed belong unto us and to our children for ever, that we may do all the words of this law.

Amos 3:7 KJV Surely the Lord God will do nothing, but he reveals his secret unto his servants the prophets.

Daniel 2:27 Daniel 2:27 NLT Daniel replied, There are no wise men, enchanters, magicians, or fortune-tellers who can reveal the king's secrets.

1 Corinthians 13:9 NLT Now our knowledge is partial and incomplete and even the gift of prophecy reveals only part of the whole picture.

Matthew 11:25 At that time Jesus answered and said, I thank thee, O Father, Lord of heaven and earth, because thou has hid these things from the wise and prudent, and has revealed them unto babes.

1 Corinthians 14:39 KJV Wherefore, brethren, covet to prophesy, and forbid not to speak with tongues.

Acts 21:9 NIV He had four unmarried daughters who prophesied.

TAU TRAIN ACTIVATE UNLEASH "THE PROPHETIC"

TAU - in Samoan and Tongan languages both mean fight or war. Train means to instruct, teach, coach, tutor, educate, ground, indoctrinate and initiate. To activate means to put in motion or make something active or operative. To unleash means to cause a strong or violent force to be released or to become unrestrained.

WHAT IS THE PROPHETIC?

The dictionary defines prophetic as accurately describing or predicting what will happen in the future or relating to or characteristic of a Prophet or prophecy.

JESUS IS PROPHECY FULFILLED

Prophecy

Isaiah 9:6 For unto us a child is born, unto us a son is given: and the government shall be upon his shoulder: and his name shall be called Wonderful, Counsellor, The Mighty God, The everlasting Father, The Prince of Peace.

Isaiah 7:14 KJV Therefore the Lord himself will give you a sign, Behold, a virgin shall conceive, and bear a son, and shall call his name Immanuel.

Fulfillment

Matthew 1:18 was found KJV Now the birth of Jesus Christ was on this wise: When as his mother Mary was espoused to Joseph, before they came together, she was found with child of the Holy Ghost.

Prophecy of Jesus the Prophet

Deuteronomy 18:15 The Lord thy God will raise up unto thee a Prophet from the midst of thee, of thy brethren, like unto me; unto him ye shall hearken

Deuteronomy 18:18 I will raise up a prophet from among their countrymen like you, and I will put My words in his mouth, and he shall speak to them all that I command you.

Fulfillment of Jesus the Prophet

Acts 3:22 KJV Moses truly said unto the fathers, A prophet shall the Lord your God raise up unto you of our brethren, like unto me; him shall ye hear in all things whatsoever he shall say unto you.

Acts 7:37 This is Moses, which said unto the children of Israel, A prophet shall the Lord your God raise up unto you of your brethren, like unto me; him shall ye hear in all things whatsoever he shall say unto you.

John 6:14 NIV After the people saw the miraculous sign that Jesus did, they began to say, "Surely this is the Prophet who is to come into the world."

John 1:45 NLT Phillip went to look for Nathanael and told him, "We have found the very person Moses and the prophets wrote about! His name is Jesus, the son of Joseph from Nazareth."

Who will prophesy?

Prophecy

Joel 2:28-29 NIV And afterward, I will pour out my Spirit upon all people. Your sons and daughters will prophesy, your old men will dream dreams, your young men will see visions. Even on my servants, both men and women, I will pour out my Spirit in those days.

Isaiah 28:11 KJV For with stammering lips and another tongue will he speak to his people.

Fulfillment

Acts 2:17-18 NIV In the last days, God says, I will pour out my Spirit on all people. Your sons and daughters will prophesy, your young men will see visions, your old men will dream dreams. Even on my servants both men and women, I will pour out my Spirit in those days, and they will prophesy.

Acts 2:4 And they were all filled with the Holy Ghost, and began to speak with other tongues, as the Spirit gave them utterance.

According to these scriptures we just read, everybody should prophesy. If you're a son or a daughter you will prophesy. King James Version reads you shall prophesy meaning future; if you haven't yet, you will and God's word does not lie if he said it surely it will come to pass.

The very next verse of scripture states on my servants, his servants those that labor in the Kingdom, those that do the work of the Lord, those that serve in the church or ministries in the communities, the servants of God are everywhere. They will prophesy. Have you ever gone somewhere and somebody said something to you that was so "on it" and then told you something about your future and you didn't even know that person? This is the hour where it's your turn and you will prophesy to people everywhere.

Joel prophesied that both men and women would prophesy. So if you have a problem with women prophesying, we can't help it. It's been spoken and written in the word of God. This prophecy covers everybody; God didn't leave anybody out in the prophetic realm and in the plan of God. Everybody will prophesy at least to some extent but not everybody is a Prophet.

CHAPTER ONE
THE PROPHETIC SEED

As long as I can remember I've always had visions and dreams and as I grew older, the interpretation of dreams. There were countless times I would tell my sisters I had seen something or sensed something bad was going to happen and when it actually did happen, I was reminded of what I told them. Sometimes I would lay awake at night afraid of the feeling that I felt and knew all too well that somebody was going to pass away. It happened with almost everybody that passed in my family including my own son Isaiah and my dad Pastor Sualua La'autuvanu Tupolo. I always knew when somebody close to my family was going to pass; I just didn't know whom it would be. At the time of course I didn't know it was a gift from God. I thought I inherited it from my family. I come from a lineage of strong women, it seemed like they were all gifted in something.

I remember as a teen I would have dreams of my close friends and myself. The dreams were warning us not to go out and hustle that day and I would call my friends and tell them. In the beginning not everybody listened and those that didn't pay attention would pay the consequences of not heeding the warning. It would unfold just how I explained it in my dream. It got to the point where my friends would call me and ask if I had a dream.

Jesus was showing me all along he was with me. Although I was doing wrong he seemed too kindly warn me through my dreams. I'm sure he knew one day I would serve him with all my heart, that one day those prayers I would pray while being chased by the undercover police, or when we were in a high speed chase would one day come to pass. I cried out and he heard my cry every time! He didn't just hear me; he answered me! That's why I love him so much! He came running to my rescue not once but countless times. I don't know why but I'm so glad he did!

Beloved I share this so you can look back and see how God's hand has been upon you in a prophetic kind of way, if that makes sense. I don't believe that we just prophesy out of the blue or we just wake up one day and we're in a prophetic dimension; I believe we were born with it in us. If you look back through your life, I'm almost positive you can relate to what I'm talking about. We are a prophetic seed and we are a prophetic generation that shall and will prophesy.

2 Timothy 1:5 KJV When I call to remembrance the unfeigned faith that is in thee, which dwelt first in thy grandmother Lois, and thy mother Eunice; and I'm persuaded that in thee also.

Definition of Unfeigned: Sincere, genuine, real, true, honest, authentic, unaffected, unpretentious, unforced, earnest, heartfelt, wholehearted, deep and from the heart

This was the kind of faith that Timothy's grandmother and mother had. This is the exact faith our ancestors had - they had unfeigned faith. I don't remember much about my grandmother Selaina Vaovasa, but I do know my grandmother was a praying woman. Every evening we would gather for prayer faithfully. This lady prayed for hours it seemed, every member in my family was mentioned in her prayers.

My grandmother was old in age and her legs were weak but she never seemed to forget the time for prayer. Although I wasn't raised with my biological mother, she was a powerful praying woman as well. I know it was their prayers that led me to Jesus and protected me all these years. I was in a life changing car accident that took place around 4am, my mother's faithful prayer time with the Lord. This blew my mind when I spent a couple of weeks with my parents and my mom woke up everyday to pray at 4am. I asked her how long has she been doing this and she said, "for years, I can't remember." I know it was her praying at the exact time of my car accident is why I am here today.

2 Timothy 1:6 KJV Wherefore I put thee in remembrance that thou stir up the gift of God, which is in thee by the putting on of my hands.

The Apostle Paul wrote this Pastoral Epistle to his son in the Lord, Timothy. It's almost as if he was saying, this will help you son; just stir up that gift. Paul was reminding him of something powerful that was in him but he obviously wasn't using it.

The gift in you is a weapon that will demolish the enemy's kingdom. Timothy must have been under some kind of spiritual attack and the Apostle Paul couldn't physically be there with him. He was telling him tap into what's in you, it's the Gift of God! Open it up, fan it, exercise it, use it and apply it.

This was an impartation from Paul to his spiritual son, as we read it's in you through the laying on of my hands. Just in case somebody may think, well I need somebody to lay hands on me; beloved all you need is to be hungry and he will fill you. I want to share something about myself. When I got filled with the gift of the Holy Ghost, I had no idea what was happening to me. I wasn't taught about the Holy Ghost even though the elder women were always speaking in tongues no one actually told me about it until after the fact. Nobody blessed me or laid hands on me nor did anybody pray for me. I went up to the altar and was praying to God. Then I fell out under the power of God and he laid hands on me. I was speaking in new tongues for about an hour I was told. I could not even get up and my husband had to help me walk! I don't mean that in a prideful way nor am I discrediting the presbytery at all. I'm just saying you don't need an ordination for the gift to be imparted in you; it is the Gift of God and it comes from God. If you are hungry you will be filled. I've also witnessed countless times when it was imparted through laying on hands of Pastors, leaders as well as the saints of God.

1 Timothy 1:18 NIV Timothy, my son, I am giving you this command in keeping with the prophecies once made about you, so that by recalling them you may fight the battle well.

Remember the prophetic word spoken over your life concerning the work of the Lord and you may fight well. If you believe them you fight well; giving up is not an option. You have visions and dreams to be fulfilled. The warfare is evidence that those prophecies are going to come to pass if we faint not.

2 Timothy 1:7 KJV For God, hath not given us the spirit of fear; but of power, and of love, and of a sound mind.

In this scripture the Apostle Paul is encouraging him and to me he's basically telling him that's not God. What are you afraid of Timothy? God gave you power over that situation. God will guard your heart to continue to love them, whoever is behind this mess or chaos. He is not the author of confusion; God has given you a sound mind. Don't be tossed to and fro; you need to be focused. You are on assignment beloved, you don't have time, stir up the gift, use the Holy Ghost power; love is powerful because God is love, and the enemy is after the love for that reason alone, for God is love. If he can take out the love he is taking out God and opens a door for him to taint the purity of the genuine anointing. Not that God is totally out of a believer but if love is not there, it leaves room for the enemy to distract, corrupt and distort with his plots and plans. All he needs is a cracked door and he will slide right on in. Shut the door and keep the devil out and if he's in there kick his butt out! You have all power and authority from Jesus. He gave it to you to do exactly that and some. Don't put up with the devil's schemes.

1 John 4:7-8 NLT Dear friends, let us continue to love one another, for love comes from God. Anyone who loves is a child of God and knows God. But anyone who does not love does not know God, for God is love.

1 John 4:18 KJV There is no fear in love; but perfect love casteth out fear: because fear hath torment. He that feareth is not made perfect in love.

Dorothy Hisatake

Chapter Two
The Birthing Place

My first encounter of a prophetic church was back in 1999. Our Youth Pastor had taken my husband and I along with the youth and young adults to visit his friends' church, Youth Pastors Ata and Lisa of Voice of Christ Church (VOC) in San Francisco. Rest in peace my sweet sister Lisa. We were still babies growing in the Lord at the time. When we stepped into VOC it was fire; the music and the worshippers were really worshipping Jesus in a way I've never seen or felt before. This church had loud music and top-notch equipment that rocked the whole neighborhood! I was excited and I loved it! I remember screaming in my husband's ear, "I told you there was more!" All we've ever known was my uncle's little church we got saved at. We had a worship team at our church but this team was on fire! We worshipped with all our hearts but this was something totally different. I didn't know at the time, but we had just entered a prophetic atmosphere.

Pastor Ata was such an awesome worship leader. He is the one that inspired my husband to sing out loud with all his heart, lead worship and flow in the prophetic. His wife Lisa would play the piano and sing prophetic worship, and at times they would both sing in their heavenly language. We were drawn to them and they were drawn to us. That would be the beginning of an awesome relationship with Ata & Lisa Tautolo and they poured into us for a season. Words cannot even express how much they helped us in the Lord. We are truly grateful for them both.

The ministers at VOC were very nice to us and they seemed eager to help us grow in the Faith. Minister Rick Uli (rest in peace), and his wife sister Mona would invite us over for dinner and of course we had Bible study first. If you knew Rick, that's the agenda; he cooked the spiritual food and his wife cooked the physical food. Brother Rick was such an awesome teacher of the word of God and he had a deep relationship with Jesus. You can feel his love for his savior - it was personal and transparent. Sister Mona was an amazing wife, mother, servant of God and I have to just say she was a great cook as well. She always had a word of encouragement for us. They were the Priscilla and Aquila of our time. I'm so grateful for those early days at the Uli residence. They both taught us so much more than they ever will know.

Then we met the Senior Pastor Pagaloa Andrew Tilo. My goodness! This older man had so much energy and fire it was contagious. He operated in the prophetic and often sang and preached at the same time; something my husband does often. It wasn't until years later we realized how prophetic worship got instilled in us, because we were still babies in the Lord during that time. We always had prophetic worship; we just didn't know that's what it was, but we would sing the song of the Lord from what was bubbling inside of us. The prophetic atmosphere and dimension we received at VOC is what pushed us into the deep. I'm so thankful Pastor Tilo is still a father to us and today we still fellowship with VOC from time to time. It is amazing that all those children back then are grown, married now and doing awesome work for the Kingdom along with their families.

You can be spiritually pregnant with purpose for months and even years. The Great Physician Jesus knows exactly what hospital you are going to deliver your baby at. In my case I was overdue. I had all the signs of a normal pregnancy. I didn't have a hunger for the things of this world. I just wanted more of Jesus and I knew there was more. I had intimacy with my savior daily, I obeyed what He said to me, I was committed to weekly events at church. I listened to my leaders but I was not in the right delivery room. I was expecting for sure but I was just waiting in the room of expectation. The dictionary defines expectation as a strong belief that something will happen or be the case in the future.

I had to go to a prophetic atmosphere to birth out the prophetic seed that was in me! We all know that in every case when a mother delivers her child, she does not stay in the hospital. Her and her baby go home as in my case. I gave birth at Voice of Christ with my midwife sister Lisa Tautolo at one of the youth gatherings and then I went home. I know now that sister Lisa was a prophetess but at the time I didn't know what that was. My baby started growing quickly - too quick that I didn't understand everything that I was experiencing. I would share them with sister Lisa and she didn't understand either, some of the things I was experiencing. I knew it was God showing me and telling me things because I was intimate with Jesus and totally surrendered to him. I knew his voice but then when I shared it with other people they didn't understand. Even my Pastor didn't understand but then the things God was telling and showing me started to manifest. I share this to say when God shows or tells you something everybody is not going to understand it because he didn't tell it to everybody. He told you and he showed you for a purpose and a reason. We must look for the revelation in every situation by searching out the matter.

Proverbs 25:2 KJV It is the glory of God to conceal a thing: but the honour of kings is to search out a matter.

Proverbs 25:2 NLT It is God's privilege to conceal things and the king's privilege to discover them.

Dorothy Hisatake

CHAPTER THREE
LIVING THE WORD

KEY SCRIPTURE

Acts 2:17-18 NIV In the last days, God says, I will pour out my Spirit on all people. Your sons and daughters will prophesy, your young men will see visions, your old men will dream dreams. Even on my servants both men and women, I will pour out my Spirit in those days, and they will prophesy.

The prophetic dimension to me is based on what is mentioned in this scripture: prophecy, visions and dreams, which I have learned that each one can tell the past, current and or the future. I found this scripture to be very helpful and a great resource in the work of the ministry as well as every area in my life. Throughout the Bible we see there were prophecies, visions and dreams. If God spoke and directed the believers in the Bible through prophecies, visions and dreams, why would he change it for us believers today? I understand we have the Bible and the early church didn't, but from the beginning of the Bible in Genesis to Revelation, we find it's filled with the prophetic dimension, prophecies, visions and dreams. Jesus is still the same yesterday, today and forever. He changes not.

After serving at my uncle's church for three years, God shifted my family in another direction. During that time my husband and I were leading the youth. He was also the worship leader and we were having revival at my uncle's church. Worship was powerful. The youth were getting filled with the spirit during worship. The church was growing but then God spoke "it's time to leave." I didn't understand it at all. My friends were coming to God and getting filled with the Spirit of God and growing spiritually. We were in the community having street services. Why would God shift us now at this moment? It didn't make sense but we followed the leading of the Spirit.

My family was praying and fasting for clarity and direction. My husband and sister both had the same dream - it had to do with us leaving to a new place. My dream was different. I dreamt we were at a bar with all these people I didn't know and we were drinking wine and eating with them. Of course in the spirit it's spiritual wine and eating the spiritual bread which of course is his word. We were in the fellowship with these believers communion with this Body of Christ.

We waited for each of us to get confirmation. We not only had the dreams but it was prophesied to my husband through a guest speaker one Sunday morning. Revelation was confirmed in the word when we gathered for Bible study. It was amazing how the three of us were so connected in the spirit to have the same dreams, even in the word of God, one of us will get a scripture in the Old Testament and one of us would get the same scripture quoted in the New Testament. We were accountable to each other and shared everything, as the spirit would reveal it to us. As I pondered on the way God was revealing his will and speaking to us I realized it was the strategies in Acts 2:17. We were actually living the word; even to what the early church did we were doing. The Early Church was our model then and it still is today. Little did I know back then that the prophetic dimension would be something normal in my life today.

God led us to San Francisco Lighthouse Church. Reluctantly I went, not because I wanted to but because of obedience to the Lord. Upon entering the doors at SF Lighthouse Church the people in my dream were sitting in the church. To my surprise the Pastor walked up to us, introduced himself and said "God told me you were coming. I prayed for help and God said help is on the way." That was really cool how God spoke to all of us concerning our situation; it was more confirmation he was with us. It was as if Jesus was saying you're going in the right path just keep going - more will unfold and it surely did. The more we grew in the Lord the more this scripture came alive to me because we were living it. This is more than a fulfillment of prophecy. This is a strategy to the church. If you apply this it surely will come alive in every area you are building; whether it's your marriage, family, church or business.

Dorothy Hisatake

CHAPTER FOUR
DO YOU KNOW
WHO YOU ARE?

On the day of Pentecost the Apostle Peter preached the first gospel message on when the 120 believers got filled with the Holy Spirit in the upper room when they were all speaking in other tongues. This is the same Peter that denied Jesus, that cut the High Priest's ear off, that went back fishing, the cocky one, the one that was cussing - yes that one! Why did God choose him? Was it his boldness or was it his faith? Jesus being prophetic and a prophet even prophesied that he was going to deny that he even knew him three times.

Matthew 26:75 Suddenly, Jesus' words flashed through Peter's mind: "Before the rooster crows, you will deny three time's that you even know me." And he went away, weeping bitterly.

When Jesus tells us to do something and we don't, have you ever experienced that, when he told you to do something and you didn't do it and when you see it manifest whatever it may be, didn't it just make you want to weep bitterly like Peter did? Beloved we really don't have time to not move on what he tells you to do concerning a certain individual. That person may be contemplating suicide and God is using you to save his or her life. Save yourself the drama and go - trust me I have been there. That is the worst feeling ever. Just step out in faith and obey him. He will lead and direct you every step of the way.

When we look at the Apostle Peter we have our own opinions as to why God would have chosen him, and we also have opinions on why he shouldn't have been chosen. Peter even confessed out of his own mouth when God filled his net with so many fishes his net couldn't contain it, he said to Jesus "depart from me for I am a sinful man." That's interesting because he obeyed Jesus and launched his net out to the deep, but it seemed like something in Peter felt he was unworthy to even be in God's presence. He just experienced the miracle he was waiting for and that was his response to Jesus. Many times our own thoughts of ourselves is what prevents us from fully walking into what God has for us. Peter had many flaws but God still chose him and it is the same for us. We are a chosen generation, a royal priesthood. Peter was chosen because he had a revelation and Jesus gave him the keys to the Kingdom of Heaven because of that revelation. It is recorded in the Bible for every believer and if we believe that revelation it grants us access to the Kingdom of Heaven as well.

THE REVELATION

Matthew 16:15-17 KJV He saith unto them, But whom say ye that I am? And Simon Peter answered and said, thou art the Christ, the Son of the living God. And Jesus answered and said unto him, Blessed art thou, Simon Bar-Jo-na: for flesh and blood hath not revealed it unto thee, but my Father which is in heaven.

Peter receives a revelation of who Jesus is, his deity - not the Son of Man the flesh, but the Son of God; God in flesh and that was by way of revelation from the Father meaning Spirit. Peter said you are the Christ the anointed one, the Messiah that was to come into the world. Jesus was saying to Peter you are blessed that you got this revelation. I don't know if Peter fully understood what that meant until the day of Pentecost when he preached to the crowds.

Matthew 16:18-19 KJV And I say also unto thee, That thou art Peter, and upon this rock I will build my church; and the gates of hell shall not prevail against it. And I will give unto thee the keys of the kingdom of heaven: and whatsoever thou shalt bind on earth shall be bound in

heaven: and whatsoever thou shalt loose on earth shall be loosed in heaven.

Jesus was saying you are absolutely right Peter, and upon that rock of revelation I will build my church. That's the church that the gates of hell will not prevail. You know who I am and I know who you are, and what you are going to say is going to build my church. You are blessed because I have given you, Peter, the keys (more than one) to unlock the Kingdom to the church. Peter you are going to tell them how to be saved and reveal my strategies to them. Any one of the disciples could have preached the first Gospel message after Jesus' ascension but only one of them had the keys meaning only one of them had the apostolic authority to first release and unlock it to the church. Once you unlock something, it is open for everybody to get in or have access to what was previously locked.

We know that keys are used to unlock, open and start something up. They are made specifically to fit a certain lock. When you insert a key into the lock you have to turn it to open or unlock it. There was a certain message that was going to be unlocked that was going to shift the whole world, the Good News of the death, the burial and the resurrection of Jesus Christ the savior of the world. The disciples including us were to be the witnesses of the Good News.

When the outpouring of the Spirit of God took place, it was the fulfillment of what was prophesied through the Prophet Joel. The Apostle Peter preached from that revelation. We see that somebody had to first prophesy it by speaking what was revealed to him by God, the revelation and the prophecy before the manifestation. It took some time but it did surely come to pass. Peter got a revelation from the Spirit letting him know exactly what was happening and then he started to build on that revelation.

Think about it: how did he know what was happening? This had never occurred before. This was the first time God's spirit was poured out in the earth. He knew by revelation the same way God revealed that Jesus was the Christ to him, back when he gave him the keys to the Kingdom. He never used the keys until the revelation met the manifestation; the key fit perfectly into the lock.

Looking back at some of Peter's journey in the Lord, we find he messed up a few times but this time I can almost sense him saying to himself "I'm not going to mess this up". In Acts Chapter 2 we read how skillful and strategic the Apostle Peter's words were. He spoke with boldness, passion, wisdom and knowledge. He started a revival fire that led to repentance. It was cutting edge, it was convicting, so much so they asked him the question: "what shall we do"? We can really see the love of God. These are the people that killed Jesus and they were the first people to hear the Good News.

Acts 2:36 NLT "So let everyone in Israel know for certain that God has made this Jesus, whom you crucified, to be both Lord and Messiah!"

Acts 2:37-38 KJV Now when they heard this, they were pricked in their heart, and said unto Peter and to the rest of the Apostles, Men and brethren, what shall we do? Then Peter said unto them, Repent, and be baptized every one of you in the name of Jesus Christ for the remission of sins, and ye shall receive the gift of the Holy Ghost.

Something was different in Peter, the way he spoke, the way he addressed the crowds he was not the same. The spirit of God will change you from denying Jesus to defending the Gospel of Jesus Christ. The Apostle Peter knew he was called to preach the Gospel and that's exactly what he did when people were mocking them. He didn't get violent like he did when he cut the high priest ear off. He spoke with confidence because he knew who he was in God. He was no longer fearful of the Jews because he was filled with the power of the Holy Ghost and he stood on the authority God gave him when he gave him the keys to the Kingdom.

Acts 2:12-15 And they were all amazed, and were in doubt, saying one to another, What meaneth this? Others mocking said, These men are full of new wine. But Peter, standing up with the eleven, lifted up his voice, and said unto them, Ye men of Judaea, and all ye that dwell at Jerusalem, be this known unto you, and hearken to my words: For these are not drunken, as ye suppose, seeing it is but the third hour of the day.

Acts 2:16-17 But this is that which was spoken by the prophet Joel; And it shall come to pass in the last days, saith God, I will pour out of my Spirit upon all flesh: and your sons and your daughters shall prophesy, and your young men shall see visions, and your old men shall dream dreams: And on my servants and on my handmaidens I will pour out in those days of my Spirit; and they shall prophesy.

_____

_____

_____

_____

_____

_____

_____

_____

_____

_____

_____

_____

_____

_____

_____

_____

_____

_____

_____

_____

Dorothy Hisatake

CHAPTER FIVE
THE PROMISE OF THE SPIRIT

The Holy Spirit is for everybody. It is the beginning of the prophetic dimension. It's where the rivers flow from the gift in you through the infilling of the Holy Spirit. Prayer will definitely stir things up just like on the day of Pentecost - as they were praying the Spirit fell and sat upon each and everyone of them and they spoke in other tongues. Some of us just need to speak out and release what's bubbling in the inside.

John 7:38-39 KJV He that believeth on me, as the scripture hath said, out of his belly shall flow rivers of living water. (But this spake he of the Spirit, which they that believe on him should receive: for the Holy Ghost was not given; because that Jesus was not yet glorified.)

Acts 1:4-5 And, being assembled together with them, commanded them that they should not depart from Jerusalem, but wait for the promise of the Father, which, saith he, ye have heard of me. For John truly baptized with water; but ye shall be baptized with the Holy Ghost not many days hence.

Acts 2:3-4 KJV And there appeared unto them cloven tongues like as of fire, and it sat upon each of them cloven tongues of fire, and it sat upon each of them. And they were all filled with the Holy Ghost, and began to speak with other tongues, as the Spirit gave them utterance.

The promise of the Father is the gift of the Holy Ghost as we just read. God wants all people; it doesn't matter what nationality, what religion, sinner or saint. God wants all people to receive the promise, even those that are far off. If it were not so, Peter would have not said it in the first sermon to the Early Church. He said it under the unction of the Holy Ghost but he didn't know God literally meant all those who are far off, meaning those who are not Jews and it even reached all of us who were once far off.

Acts 2:39 This promise is to you, to your children, and to those far away all who have been called by the Lord our God.

Definition of promise: A declaration or assurance that one will do a particular thing or that a particular thing will happen.

We also find that 3,000 people received the word and obeyed it right on the spot. Peter spoke with great conviction and the people felt something they never felt before. They felt the Spirit that was in Peter and the rest of the 120 that gathered in the upper room.

Acts 2:41 KJV Then they that gladly received his word were baptized: and the same day there were added unto them about three thousand souls.

The same people that heard the gospel message and obeyed it continued in the fellowship and learned from the Apostles who Jesus commissioned and sent as his witnesses, after they received the power from the Holy Ghost.

Acts 1:8 KJV But ye shall receive power, after that the Holy Ghost is come upon you: and ye shall be witnesses unto me both in Jerusalem, and in all Judaea, and in Samaria, and unto the uttermost part of the earth.

Acts 2:42 KJV And they continued steadfastly inn the apostles; doctrine and fellowship, and in breaking of bread, and in prayers.

The very first church submitted to their leaders, the Apostles. They didn't just get baptized and leave, they stayed in fellowship with the believers, prayers and in the word of God.

Definition of Steadfast: resolutely or dutifully firm and unwavering

The first believers were not double minded. They were committed and obedient to the Gospel of Jesus Christ and they stood firm on the foundation of the Prophets, Apostles, and Jesus Christ being the Chief Cornerstone.

_____

_____

_____

_____

_____

_____

_____

_____

_____

_____

_____

_____

_____

_____

_____

_____

_____

_____

_____

_____

_____

CHAPTER SIX
OBEDIENCE OVER FEAR

Looking at the story of Saul, we see Ananias a disciple who was in the same city as Saul, was having a vision and the Lord Jesus was speaking to him regarding Saul who was persecuting the Christians at the time.

Acts 9:11-12 KJV And the Lord said unto him, Arise, and go into the street which is called Straight, and enquire in the house of Judas for one called Saul, of Tarsus: for behold, he prayeth, And hath seen in a vision a man named Ananias coming in, and putting his hand on him, that he might receive his sight.

Acts 9:15 KJV But the Lord said unto him, Go thy way: for he is a chosen vessel unto me, to bear my name before the Gentiles, and Kings, and the Children of Israel;

Here is the prophecy concerning Saul. We see there was a vision given to both of them regarding each other. We see clear directions from the Lord but what is amazing is Ananias's obedience to the Lord. He heard how Saul was persecuting the Christians but that did not stop him. If we are going to act on what God shows us we can't be doubtful or fearful.

Acts 9:17-18 NLT And Ananias went and found Saul. He laid his hands on him said, "Brother Saul, the Lord, who appeared to you on the road, has sent me so that you might regain your sight and be filled with the Holy Spirit." Instantly something like scales fell from Saul's eyes, and he regained his sight. Then he got up and was baptized.

Even Saul who is also called Paul had to obey what Peter preached. When Ananias laid his hands on him he was filled with the gift of the Holy Ghost. Then he got up and was baptized. That was so important to Jesus that he spoke to Ananias in a vision and then sent him over there to a man that was persecuting the Christians!

Jesus told Ananias that Paul was his chosen vessel to the Gentiles, but we find out as we continue to read in the Book of Acts the story of Cornelius - the first Gentile non-Jewish family to receive salvation, and that it wasn't Paul that was sent but it was Peter that was sent to his house from instructions he received in a vision from the Lord. We see again the prophetic dimension in operation.

The Apostle Peter was sent because he was the one that had the keys. Once he unlocked or opened the Gospel to the gentiles, the Apostle Paul was able to go in and preach the death, the burial and the resurrection of Jesus Christ all throughout the world.

Peter would not have stepped foot in Cornelius's house if the Lord didn't speak directly to him in a vision. What Peter didn't know is that Cornelius had a vision about him just the day before.

You can read the full story in Acts chapter 10 of how Peter was sent on an assignment by Jesus himself.

Acts 10:44-45 NIV While Peter was still speaking these words, the Holy Spirit came on all who heard the message. The circumcised believers who had come with Peter were astonished that the gift of the Holy Spirit had been poured out even on Gentiles.

How did they know they were filled with the Holy Spirit?

Acts 10:46 NIV For they heard them speaking in tongues and praising God.

Acts 10:47-48 KJV Can any man forbid water, that these should not be baptized, which have received the Holy Ghost as well as we? And he commanded them to

baptized in the name of the Lord. Then prayed they him to tarry certain days.

Peter didn't know what to do or how to act so he went back to the beginning when they got filled on the day of Pentecost and followed the pattern of God. Peter also proclaimed to them: I see God is not a respecter of persons. God will fill whom he chooses.

I witnessed people that were hung over, smelling like alcohol and marijuana get filled with the Holy Spirit with speaking with tongues. Whatever was going on with these folks God looked at the heart. It all begins with repentance. I know those individuals repented and God filled them with his Spirit. We cannot judge from the outer appearance because God looks past that and into the heart and soul of man.

I'll share one story on this topic. I picked up a sister named Lisa also known as Lisa Bam Bam for church. She was hung over, I insisted that she still come to church and I wasn't leaving without her. During the service as the Pastor preached I looked over and seen her crying all through the sermon. The Pastor did an altar call and there was Lisa front and center. She got filled that day with the Spirit of God and was speaking in other tongues. That day changed me, what kind of God is this? I asked myself. There were lots of people at the altar that wanted to get filled with the Spirit but the one you least expect was the one that had an encounter with the living God. Sister Lisa went on to be with the Lord but I'm so glad she was born again in water and Spirit!

Dorothy Hisatake

CHAPTER SEVEN
THE PROPHETIC CALL

In reading the Book of Acts we find that the insight, instructions, revelations, dreams and visions were given for a purpose and that was to bring the Good News as well as the gift of the Holy Ghost to those believers. It's the same way today. God wants to give his Holy Spirit to every believer. There's nothing wrong if you believe, that's great but there is more, the prophetic dimension and that is what's missing. It's time for us to be refilled, revived, renewed and restored.

Referring back to the Key Scripture of Acts 2:17, if everybody is a son or a daughter that will prophesy, then there should be some out of them that are called to be Prophets.

There are many Prophets in the Old Testament. Let's take a look at the Prophet Jeremiahs' call. He was young and didn't have a clue to the prophetic but he was still called. Let all the Jeremiahs rise up in this hour!

The Prophet Jeremiah's Call

Jeremiah 1:5 NLT "I knew you before I formed you in your mother's womb. Before you were born I set you apart and appointed you as my prophet to the nations."

God knew us before he formed us; it was the Creator himself that formed us in the belly. So creativity is in us, which is part of being prophetic. We were set apart and appointed, yes like Jeremiah. He was a Prophet but it doesn't exclude us. We are still a prophetic people. Jeremiah was called to the nations; we are called to our communities, schools and families and if God wills we will be in the nations too. This world is so diverse we are surrounded by many nations!

Before we even knew God he had already set us apart for his glory and his purpose. We exist because he wills that we exist. I declare we live and we shall not die until we accomplish what we were created to do in the earth.

Jeremiah 1:6 KJV Then said I, Ah, Lord God! Behold, I cannot speak: for I am a child.

Jeremiah 1:9 KJV Then the LORD put forth his hand, and touched my mouth. And the LORD said unto me, Behold, I have put my words in thy mouth.

God will put his words in our mouths. We are his witnesses, his servants and his children. Fear will always make excuses. Doubt will keep you wavering to and fro without ever stepping out on anything. Jeremiah said I can't speak and I'm just a child. This is the time for the Jeremiah's to rise and boldly speak the word of the Lord. How many Jeremiah's are sitting in the church pews, that have no idea about the prophetic dimension. We can't blame them if we never created a prophetic culture in our gatherings.

Jeremiah 1:11-12 NLT Then the LORD said to me, "Look, Jeremiah! What do you see?" And I replied, "I see a branch from an almond tree." And the LORD said, "That's right, and it means that I am watching, and I will certainly carry out all my plans.

It's interesting to me that God asked Jeremiah, what do you see, and then there was another vision, and God asked him again what do you see? And then after that the instructions to the vision, that's the prophetic dimension. That is how we activate our young people by asking them what do you see. They might be seeing things but nobody is asking them the question.

We've learned that we have to give them an opportunity by asking them if they seen, heard or felt anything. When we started asking the youth questions they answered and every time it has always been lined up to what was actually going on during that time. Or it was giving us insight and deeper revelation to what God was doing or speaking to us. It's really exciting when the body of Christ is connected in the spiritual realm and using the spiritual gifts to edify and build each other up. We see in the Bible that's exactly who the gifts were for, the body of Christ to build up the church in their purpose in God.

Ephesians 4:7-8 NLT However, he has given each one of us a special gift through the generosity of Christ. That is why the scriptures say, "When he ascended to the heights, he led a crowd of captives and gave gifts to his people."

Ephesians 4:11-12 NLT Now these are the gifts Christ gave to the church: the apostles, the prophets, the evangelists, and the pastors and teachers. Their responsibility is to equip God's people to do his work and build up the church, the body of Christ.

1 Corinthians 12:7 NLT A spiritual gift is given to each of us so we can help each other.

1 Corinthians 12:8-12 KJV For to one is given by the Spirit the word of wisdom; to another the word of knowledge by the same Spirit; To another faith by the same Spirit; to another the gifts of healing by the same Spirit. To another the working of miracles; to another prophecy; to another discerning of spirits; to another divers kinds of tongues; to another the interpretation of tongues: But all these worketh that one and the selfsame Spirit, dividing to every man severally as he will. For as the body is one, and hath many members, and all the members of that one body, being many, are one body: so also is Christ.

There are many parts to one body, not only in our local church but also as a whole. If we can put down the names of our churches and function together as one body, how pleasing that would be to Jesus!

Dorothy Hisatake

Chapter Eight
Benefits Of The Prophetic

10 Benefits of the Prophetic Dimension

- It gives us warning

- It gives us direction & guidance

- It foresees into the future

- It helps to prepare you

- It brings healing & restoration

- It confirms what God is doing

- It releases the mind & heart of God

- It sees the plans of the enemy before an attack

- It causes repentance

- It builds you up

The prophetic helps us in so many ways, it helps even more when your circle of friends, family or church are prophetic because each one can operate in anyway of these things I listed. One can have a word to build up and one can see where the enemy is lurking and so on. It really is a benefit to the Kingdom and its citizens.

All through the Bible from Genesis to Revelation we see these benefits. If the prophetic helped those in the Bible times, then surely it will help us in our everyday lives and to wage a good warfare in these last and evil days.

10 Things That The Prophetic Is Not

- It does not judge

- It is not spooky

- It is not hidden, secret or private

- It is not rude or prideful

- It does not embarrass people

- It does not tear people down

- Is not fortune telling

- It does not lie

- It does not boast

- It does not bring up your past to

shame you but to free you

It is important to make sure your prophetic gifts are submitted to the man or woman of God, to those who are in authority. It should always flow from a pure heart and in love. If there is rebellion, pride and wounds that are not healed, there is room for witchcraft and error. I believe that is how witchcraft creeps into the church because gifts that are not submitted to God, and to those in authority. Rebellion and pride does not want anyone to tell them anything. Those spirit hates submission and it's very dangerous to a believers walk. Rebellion is defined in the dictionary as an act of violent or open resistance to an established government or ruler. Just like in our country it is the same in the Kingdom of God. There's a government and rules just like the laws of the land. We must abide by those rules and laws or we will have to pay the penalty for breaking them.

Dorothy Hisatake

_____

_____

_____

_____

_____

_____

_____

_____

_____

_____

_____

_____

_____

_____

_____

_____

_____

_____

_____

_____

CHAPTER NINE
PROPHETIC ACTIVATIONS

Here are some things we did to activate the prophetic in our churches and gatherings. Of course everybody has their own style and will move as the Spirit of God will lead, but as the rivers start to flow out of the belly of the church it will be hard to stop! The belly is the core. The leadership, if it hits there, it will flow from the head to the toes meaning even the little babies will prophesy.

In the Church Service

Praying in the spirit is always going to open up the door to the prophetic dimension in the church. The atmosphere has to be one of true worship not perfection with the voices and music, just truth and from the heart. Sometimes we focus too much on sounding good when Jesus just wants a heart of worship, not a voice of worship.

Communication is important and the body of Christ should work and flow together in unity. When we gather for prayer with the core team before service, we briefly share what God has been showing everybody. It can be that morning or that week, then we pray for how God wants us to strategize the service applying what each member had seen. I believe this is where the enemy tries to attack at the most, the unity of the believers. We can see and hear a whole lot if we were connected spiritually. We need to shift from the normalcy of the traditional church and exercise freedom in the Spirit, for where the Spirit of the Lord is there is freedom.

When the atmosphere is high with praise and worship and it's descending, that is usually the best time to step out and see how God leads. Sometimes the minstrels will just play, flowing non-stop and the singers have all silenced, that is a good time to make up a song of the Lord. Sometimes you have to sing what's bubbling in you, sing what you want to see or what God is doing. Sometimes we sing and prophesy. The Bible says sing unto the Lord a new song. This can also be a time to release the prophetic word to the church. We have to make room for it in the service. If we move too quickly or in a rush to move to the next thing without waiting on the Lord, we can miss something God wants to say or do.

The prophetic is fresh and new. It's exciting and refreshing. The worst thing is singing the same old songs and nothing new is bursting forth. That makes the church comfortable and sometimes we can just be going through the motions. Worship should lead to deliverance and repentance.

As the church moves in the dimension or the flow of the prophetic, it should be led by the leader that is most familiar with the prophetic which is usually the apostles and prophets or those that prophesy. The evangelists, pastors and teachers will be aligned as well. As they all flow with the move of God the rest of the church will all start to shift together. I've never really experienced when it was not of God because we don't try to make it happen if there is no unction of the Spirit. We only operate in it if the rivers are flowing from the worship or prayers. If there is resistance it is best to wait until every wall and distraction is torn down.

Once you step out you start by saying what you seen, heard or felt in the spirit. Then ask if anybody else seen or heard anything? Yes of course they did and they will share it if they are obedient and then that revelation will be the rock you are building on for that season. I can't tell you how many times this has happened. It has either bought more understanding to the word that was preached, or sometimes it brings a whole new word to the body and everybody will build on that. Even outside of church you will see that word manifest all through out the week and sometimes longer. Revelation is so deep because once you get one you never forget it. So it will be used and will be reminded from time to time through your walk in the Lord.

Many times when we do this with the body of Christ, there will be some of those who can see where the enemy is attacking, which is so powerful because you can stop the attack by prayer before it happens and once you're in prayer more things will be revealed from that one rock of revelation. Again communication is key. That's why the gates of hell will not prevail because this is the church that builds on revelation not just on who Jesus is but what he's saying to the church. He speaks to everybody not one person will be left out if they are open they will hear or see something in the spirit. That's why we are a body we work together not alone. We are accountable to each other and we share everything in common just like the early church. It's normal for two or three to see the same vision know that God is establishing it.

We've experienced times when a whole ministry was birthed out from the prophetic. I will share one time with you, we had a guest speaker on Pentecost Sunday May 2016 named Pastor Del and he operates in the prophetic. After Pastor Del preached he was prophesying on a few people than he called for my husband and I. He said something to us that only God knew because God was the one who told us what Pastor Del said to us. He said a lot of things but one thing he said was really on it. He said "God is going to use you to plant churches, and you need to start dreaming of where you're going to plant these churches." The amazing thing is we were already having dreams and cities would pop up in prayer; one specifically was Sacramento, California. Now this is where obedience had to kick in which it did and the very next month in June we launched a church in Sacramento and then in July we packed up and moved our family there. Today we have two churches there; one in the North and one in the South.

In The Home

Prayer is the doorway to the prophetic in the home. Most Polynesians were raised in praying homes. It is our culture and the way of our ancestors. Praying together as a family is powerful, especially when you're praying in unity for each other's needs and for the needs of the family. Prayer can always go deeper no matter what level we are on. Spirit led prayers opens up the door for breakthrough, deliverance and healing. Sometimes we might have to war in the spirit together for somebody else's breakthrough.

The way I discovered to activate your children is to have them involved by asking them often did they dream, see, hear or feel anything. We pray together then ask questions and then we randomly pick one of our kids to read the Bible to wherever they are led to and just start reading. This is the exciting part because they see God speaking and confirming everything through his word.

If there are certain needs, pray for strategies for the needs individually and then share with the individual what each person got from the Spirit. That helps the person so much in whatever they may be going through. If the individual is not there then build upon the revelation. God may use you to help the individual and bring them into deliverance, healing or restoration.

Sometimes we might have to turn the lights off and blast the music and get in some personal prayer time with the Lord. It's more intimate and you can hear more clearly that way sometimes.

In Bible Study

When we give Bible study to families we usually teach on whatever the topic is then after, we will share our key scripture Acts 2:17. We make it a point to share this scripture because it is what they are supposed to do according to the scripture. We always leave room for them to exercise their gifts. When starting off you will not understand what you see but there will be those that will help you grow and have the understanding of what you see. If the gifts are to build, encourage and edify the body of Christ, then everything we need is in the body of Christ. That's why communication is vital.

During this time I ask them have you ever had visions? Have you had any dreams? Most of the time it's a no, or regarding dreams they don't remember and if they did I ask them if they wanted to share it. As you grow in the prophetic dimension you will also grow in the gifts, interpretations of dream and revelations will just come naturally. There are many gifted people but they just don't know their gifts just yet, it has to be unlocked meaning opened.

Since I have permission I'll share a time I gave the Tolo Family who are members of the church Bible study. I did everything I just mentioned, when they told me they never had visions I created an atmosphere for the prophetic to be activated in them. You must have a desire to see the prophetic gift stirred up in people or you will not push for it to come to pass in them.

I pulled a chair up and asked one of them to sit down as the person was seated, I then asked everybody to stretch forth their hands to pray for the individual and ask God to give them visions.

Each child sat and got prayed for and each person had a turn to say what they seen or felt and guess what? Each one of them had visions, a word or something. They were so excited because some of us seen the same thing.

It was amazing because some of us seen way into their future and when we shared it they were amazed that God showed them visions of what they already knew they wanted to become or something that was lined up.

Savannah who is seventeen years of age and the oldest of the five children, I would say was the strongest in the prophetic, meaning she had the most insight. Maybe because she was born a worshipper; as a little girl she was singing praises to God and singing on the worship team. Before the night was over she was prophesying to her siblings like she's been doing it forever. She was on fire!

Her parents Junior and Elaine were filled with joy as they seen their children operate in the prophetic along with them. It was beautiful to witness. Every last one in the Tolo family even the youngest, Serenity who is ten years old was prophesying! I've witnessed these children get filled with the spirit, and share their visions and prophesy. They are definitely prophetic worshippers and a prophetic company!

Group Meetings

When we meet for Bible study with the church we do the same thing but only those that want prayer come up and we make sure the youth are involved. Some of them see visions, others prophesy and some get a word of knowledge. I can say when they prayed for me they were on point and it helped give me some direction as well as confirmation. This opens up the window for them to start to see visions, dreams, insight and revelations. Nothing is hidden, it's all brought to the light and we all share our thoughts on the visions and so on. We are accountable to each other; everything is open and nothing is done in the dark. Unless it's something personal and might embarrass the person, in that case yes but still share it with whoever is in authority because God will give them what revelation is needed to set them free. We all build together in unity.

I recall on one Saturday evening prayer meeting I wanted the youth to experience the prophetic so I asked each child to let us pray for them and PJ who walked in late just jumped right in and started praying for his sister. PJ seen a vision that shocked him and made him step back he said "whoa I just seen a white bird," I explained it was a dove symbolic to the Spirit of God and peace of God. I went on to tell the youth that God was going to do something in the youth. The next day at church one of the youth, Samson who is 14 years old came up for prayer. The Holy Spirit came upon him and he was filled with the spirit and was speaking in other tongues. He could not stop speaking in tongues. Everybody stopped what they were doing to witness Samson speak in his heavenly language.

It's so amazing witnessing the youth operate in the Prophetic, it's pure and authentic. In San Francisco No Limits there is a 10-year old named LJ this boy always has a Word for the church and is not afraid to speak up. He knows his gift. There is something about when you know! The more you keep prophesying and opening it up for others to step out the more people will began to shift and that's what creates the prophetic culture.

When you gather together and you are closing out in prayer in a circle you can also activate the prophetic during the prayer. Before you link up you let the group know if they see or hear anything, to let you or whoever is leading out know what they see, feel or hear. Sometimes they will tell you right there or they will tell you after the prayer but always ask the question. We usually just call it out as we're all praying together and then we shift to the leading of what was being called. It could be a family member of somebody in the church. When everybody is praying together for that need out loud it's more powerful because everybody is focusing on that one thing in unity. If this is new to them you have to keep asking before and after prayer until they know how to flow in it.

When you are moving into the prophetic dimension do it together so everybody is learning together and it's more effective when you all are communicating to one another. Communication and unity are very powerful weapons of the church. When we communicate we are well informed and we are not in the dark. We know what's going on and we are all on the same page. The Holy Spirit did not fall until they were all in one mind and one accord.

Dorothy Hisatake

Chapter Ten
Building Prophetic Teams

When building or forming prophetic teams the leader should be the one God put in authority like the Pastor or Apostle until the leader feels to appoint somebody else but even then he or she still needs to be aware of everything. Let us not keep anything hidden from our leaders because that is what Satan likes to do: sneak, hide, do things secretly, and operate in darkness. Operating in darkness is not of God, and opens the door to the enemy. If the group is really prophetic they will find out anyway. Leaders are anointed to help guide you and push you to your purpose. God gives his leaders wisdom to help his people.

It is important to know what gifts are in the group so that way when things start to be revealed you know who is more gifted in that area and you submit to the leading until you all start to get revelation from that rock. It will move fast, revelation upon revelation. You will then have something to build on to advance the Kingdom and destroy the works of the enemy and more. It will surely be revealed to each and everybody in the team. You will see the signs all over. It could be a license plate, a billboard, a sign on a bus or wall are examples. You will even hear it being preached but you will see it because God wants you to see it so he will show you over and over, especially so you don't forget. The Spirit will also give scriptures to somebody in the team.

Stay in unity and if there is anything that is not of God in you repent and remove it and replace it with one of the fruits of the spirit. An example is if you have hatred. Renounce it by saying, I command you hatred to go and I release love to fill me, in Jesus name. Keep in mind if it's hatred or whatever spirit it may be, it is also attached to other spirits so just be led by the

Holy Ghost. He will direct you as well as expose what is not of God. Forgive others and ask for forgiveness if you need to. Just don't delay; do it as soon as possible so you can move on without it haunting you later. Unforgiveness will keep you stuck.

Our prophetic teams are always in communication with our visions, dreams, and word of knowledge or insight on something. We are a team that works, prays and fast together but not necessarily physically together. We know we are on assignment to stop every plot and plan the enemy is scheming up against our families, churches and communities. Whatever way of communication fits your group; get it together as soon as possible. We do this and we have witnessed how powerful and effective it is. You will notice the difference. We can pray but when you have the prophetic dimension, you see, feel or hear what you need and that gives you the strategies and what to pray for and what's coming against us, as opposed to just praying. Seeing is a weapon in the spirit. When you can see what's going on, the enemy doesn't stand a chance. That's the church that the gates of hell will not prevail because revelation is knowledge and insight.

The core group is the frontline of the prophetic dimension in our church gatherings. You don't need a whole lot of people and if you don't have any prophetic people just raise up whom you have. We are always looking to impart and raise up more people; we can never have enough. We love to see people operate in their gifts.

When we planted another church in Sacramento in the South side, we didn't really have a lot of people because it was a new work. Pastor "P" and his wife First Lady Lili would come out and help us. First Lady Lili was starting to step out in the prophetic realm and that night I was at the altar praying for a young lady that had a lot of hurt. As I was praying for her I didn't feel anything breaking, it was just cold. I continued praying for her, just trying to get through the wall. I felt her hurt and pain but she was not releasing anything, just blank. As I was praying what should I do, just then First Lady Lili walked up to me and whispered in my ear "I got walk." Wisdom came with the word so I grabbed the young lady's hands and I said "come on we're walking out of your past," and we started to walk around the church. With every step, I called out something in her past that had her bound. As soon as she took the first step she broke out in tears. If First Lady Lili did not step out and share the word she got, that young lady would not have gotten a breakthrough. It might not make sense to you but just share it with those in authority or the one that is praying for the individual. God gave it to you for a reason. It is for somebody's healing and deliverance.

On the third service in south Sacramento, we had some new members and we wanted to activate them in the prophetic and we also wanted to activate our little children. We have a lot of young children and it can get crazy so I had all of them sit in the front row during worship since their parents are in the worship team. I told them we were going to use them during the service.

It was offering time and I called them all up to the stage, my son, my nephew and nieces are familiar with the prophetic so we were activating the new children these children are generational babies. Their grandfather is a Pastor and their parents were raised in church. I asked the adults if we could have a volunteer so the children can pray. I then told them listen for God to speak to you, and he will give you a vision or a word. All the children received a vision or a word from the Lord.

Evangelist Dora volunteered for the children to pray for her. I prayed with them then waited for a minute or so, then I asked them what did they get. I went down the line; Julius "Juju" told her, "I seen you on a stage a light was shining so bright on you and people were bowing down." Evangelist Dora has a powerful message of deliverance from what she's been delivered from. The anointing on her life has led people to repentance. So Julius's (Juju) vision, of course confirmed to her that she needed to stay on assignment. I also want to add that Juju is only seven years old. He's been prophesying since five. One child got the word Faith; each one got something to share with Evangelist Dora. As the children continued telling her, she was in amazement and in tears. Something about when the younger sons and daughters prophesy, it's so pure and innocent. That's why we start training them when they are young and that's why the enemy starts his attacks on them at an early age. He is fully aware that we are a prophetic generation.

Next another sister steps up for prayer and Israel (Izzy), was standing right next to me. As all the children are telling her what they got, Izzy is tapping me so I turn to her and she whispers to me, I heard "Blood Issue." Now this baby is only five years old and there is no way she is going to know this word. Her parents had not been in church for a while so it had to be God speaking through her. She went on to mention to me about the sisters siblings so we all started praying for her siblings.

I asked Zion, Izzy's brother what's the word? He looks at us and says "passion" but he pronounced it like "paaaaasssioon." It was the cutest thing because you know it was the first time he ever used that word. Izzy is our little prophetess. She randomly just tells me to pray for certain people out of the blue. One time her parents Mana and Michael, were on their way to church blasting their gospel music and praying in the spirit, Izzy starts yelling "turn the music down! Turn the music down!" Her parents look at her like ok. As they turn down the music, Izzy proceeds to tell them, "God spoke to me. He said he's moving all the clouds so the kids don't get sick." So her mom shares the story with the church, but that night the altar was packed with youth and young adults. They were getting their breakthroughs and healing was taking place. They were crying, hugging each other and really getting touched by the Lord. As I looked at the youth I was reminded of Izzy's words. God moved the clouds so the youth can get their healing. Izzy only could explain the way a 5-year old would.

Her mother Mana has been our spiritual daughter since she was a teenager she is now thirty years old. We baptized her and helped her grow in her walk. As a teen she was on fire for God, a drummer, a worshipper and a praise dancer. Then her family moved and we didn't see her as much and as the years passed, we lost touch with her. I had a dream in 2000 when I was attending my uncle's church. In my dream we were at a church function and somebody gave me a plate it was a big Polynesian plate that comes in a box, the plate had all the traditional poly food but the Taro. In my dream I was making a big deal about the Taro missing. I asked people, "where is the Taro?" Nobody answered me about the Taro missing. As I woke up I looked at the dream spiritually. Ok to be honest, there's lots of things missing in our Polynesian churches. I say Polynesian because my plate was a Poly plate. In my dream it was a big deal to me that the Taro was missing and I remember thinking, that's all it needs and the plate would be complete. Years after the dream in 2012, Mana came to our church in San Francisco and she tells my husband and I, "I have somebody I want you to meet, my boyfriend. He proposed to me but I told him I needed my spiritual parents' approval, so here he is. Michael these are my spiritual parents Eighi and Dorothy." Ok so I'm thinking, how does this girl expect us to give our approval; we just met this guy. So being prophetic I ask her "ok tell us one thing about him just one thing anything that comes to your mind." She pauses for a minute then she states to me, "well he made me some Taro." I said, "Oh my God, Michael is the Taro!" I didn't even know how deep that was back then but I told her my dream and we gave our approval. Today their family is serving the Lord with us and Michael is fluent in Samoan, which is his first language my husband and I are not fluent in Samoan so he brings the Taro to the plate if you understand what I mean. I had the dream before I met Mana, then years later in 2012 she shows up at our church with Michael and then again in October 2018 she shows up at the first service and they've been serving with us since. That's what I mean when I say the prophetic dimension goes a long way.

After we activated the youth, the adults were next. Most of the new members present that night never had visions but before the night was over they were having visions and they were so free. When I say free I mean these new members were making songs up. Another member just went up and started playing the guitar. He played a little back in High School but Michael was flowing like he was a professional musician and his brother was singing songs from his heart with his own words.

Our prophetic teams bring different things to the table so that is what makes it so powerful and effective. I'll give an example of one of our teams. Sister Carol has a lot of dreams. Her dreams bring awareness and direction to certain situations. Prophetess Regina sees visions all through the day. You can have a conversation with her and mention something and she will literally have a vision as you are talking to her. She is also a prayer warrior, more so because she sees where the enemy is attacking. Our gifts go hand in hand; it's amazing! Evangelist Dora has understanding of numbers and her insight is profound. The Pastors have the revelation of the word of God. We often have the same word but in different locations. It is normal in our churches. When the leaders are prophetic the whole church will be prophetic. Everything we need is in his body of believers.

We have many more prophetic people, too many to name, who also share their dreams, visions and insight. Many of them will get just one word and we will search that one word out. We look up the definition, and search for it in the Bible, we don't take the prophetic dimension lightly because we know how valuable it is in the Kingdom of God. We place so much importance on the prophetic that all the youth, young adults and little babies are all taught the prophetic and given the opportunity to step out in faith as the spirit leads them.

Acts 2:39 KJV For the promise is unto you, and to your children, and to all that are afar off, even as many as the Lord our God shall call.

My son Malaki just recently had a daughter and the week before in church at San Francisco we were having a revival service and during the prophetic flow my nephew Xavier said he seen a waterfall. My friend, brother Nick who was visiting messaged me and said "You know I kept thinking about the kid that said he seen a waterfall, well waterfalls make rainbows and that's God's promise." See that scripture Acts 2:39? The promise is for you and your children! So building on this Xavier has a vision, remember our Key Scripture Acts 2:17, brother Nick receives a revelation: waterfalls make rainbows, which is the promise, and I got the word Acts 2:39. When my grandbaby was born, as her mother was pushing her out, all the water probably from her water bag was bursting forth but my granddaughters head was right there so all the water splashed up making a waterfall. My son looked at me and said "Xavier's word." We all got wet including the doctors. Where there is revelation there will be manifestation. This all lined up perfectly with the word in Acts 2:39. I want to add another thing about the waterfall, this week I was taking my other son Judah to school and I was in the car praying in the spirit. I looked up and there were some workers doing something in the ground and as we passed all this water came springing forth from the ground creating a big waterfall that was spilling onto the streets. I felt the Lord was reminding me about his promise. Judah and I looked at each other and started laughing because we both knew it was a sign from God.

One thing that we make a point to do with our youth, young adults and babies is tell them they are part of the 5-fold ministry so it's embedded in them at a young age so as they grow, their gift and calling grows with them. My son Jabez who just turned ten years old, from a baby he was told he's a prophet so he just flows with it. He loves the prophetic and is always eager to hear and learn more about it. This boy loves to give his insight and revelations when we're talking about dreams. I often have him pray with me to see what he feels and he always has a word to help me in that moment. Jabez is the son I prophesied about having, my daughter was five at the time and I started telling everybody at church I was going have one more baby. I even told my goddaughter Raven to save all her newborn babies clothes and shoes for me because I was going to have one more baby. Sure enough I got pregnant!

I remember one time we were praying for one of the youth; his name is Isaiah. On that same day we were telling the youth they are part of the five fold ministry gifts and I was telling him, "you are a prophet." As soon as I said it, his mother Daffy who was also praying with us said "oh my goodness I just seen the words prophet written all over his face". Out of the mouths of two or three witnesses let every word be established. Sure enough the next week after Bible study, we were praying and Isaiah was prophesying and having visions; he was on fire and really excited. Keep it moving Prophet Isaiah!

I have so many stories I can tell you about what we discovered in the prophetic dimension. I don't know if there is a right way or wrong way but this is what we did and continue to do and we have seen tremendous results. We didn't have anybody to teach us how to move in the prophetic. We relied on the Holy Ghost and he taught us. We also learned from each other and stepped out on what we felt God was telling us to do. There was a time when we didn't use the prophetic as much and looking back at that season, I surely wish we did. There were some things that could have been prevented and I definitely would have been warned of things before hand, because the prophetic tells you the future so you can prepare for things. PLEASE keep that in mind.

We can see all through the Book of Acts every move of God began with prayer. I pray this book has been a blessing to you. May all your spiritual senses come alive as you step into the prophetic realm. I pray it blesses you in the same way it has blessed our families and our ministries. In Jesus Name, Amen.

1 Samuel 10:6 KJV And the Spirit of the LORD will come upon thee and thou shalt prophesy with them, and shalt be turned into another man.

Ephesians 2:19 KJV And are built upon the foundation of the apostles and prophets, Jesus Christ himself being the chief corner stone.

Acts 2:17-18 KJV And it shall come to pass in the last days, saith God, I will pour out of my Spirit upon all flesh: your sons and daughters shall prophesy, and your young men shall see visions, and your old men shall dream dreams: And upon my servants and my handmaidens I shall pour out in those days of my Spirit and they shall prophesy

1 Corinthians 14:1 KJV Follow after charity, and desire spiritual gifts, but rather that ye may prophesy.

1 Corinthians 14: 31 KJV For ye may all prophesy one by one, that all may learn, and all may be comforted.

1 Corinthians 14:39 KJV Wherefore, brethren, covet to prophesy and forbid not to speak with tongues.

Revelation 10:11 KJV And he said unto me, Thou must prophesy again before many peoples, and nations, and tongues, and kings.

Dorothy Hisatake

_____

_____

_____

_____

_____

_____

_____

_____

_____

_____

_____

_____

_____

_____

_____

_____

_____

_____

_____

_____

Dorothy Hisatake

To order other books by Dorothy Hisatake

Email us at TrainActivateUnleash@gmail.com

Website: www.TAUtrainactivateunleash.com

Or visit our Facebook Page at TrainActivateUnleash

E-BOOKS

TAU THE EVANGELIST Volume I

TAU THE EVANGELIST Volume II

BOOKS

TAU THE PROPHETIC Volume I

TAU THE PROPHETIC Volume II

Made in the USA
Middletown, DE
10 January 2023

21619175R00047